# Dear Calendula

## Love Poems to Plants

CARLI ANNE WOLF

Few are those who see with their
own eyes and feel with their
own hearts.

ALBERT EINSTEIN

# Table of Contents

# Bloodroot

Family: Papaveraceae
Genus:Sanguinaria
Species: S. canadensis

I unabashedly unfold,
releasing my potent beauty.

Bloodroot beauty, make
Red blood redder.
Strengthen my heart,
And numb my mind.
Bloodroot beauty,
Paint for war.
Red blood grow redder,
Strengthen my heart,
And numb the pain.
Bloodroot beauty,
Paint for war.
Red blood grow redder,
Numb the pain of
This strengthening heart.

# Borage

Family: Boraginaceae
Genus: Borago
Species: B. officinalis

I know joy, because I know
forgiveness.

Drink me in.
Make me giddy with your presence.
Get me drunk on your courage.
Show me joy and love,
Then teach me of forgiveness.
Breathe me out.
Take to my lungs and inhale.
Touch me where I cannot reach.
Heal me and I bow.
Release never tasted so sweet.

# Calendula

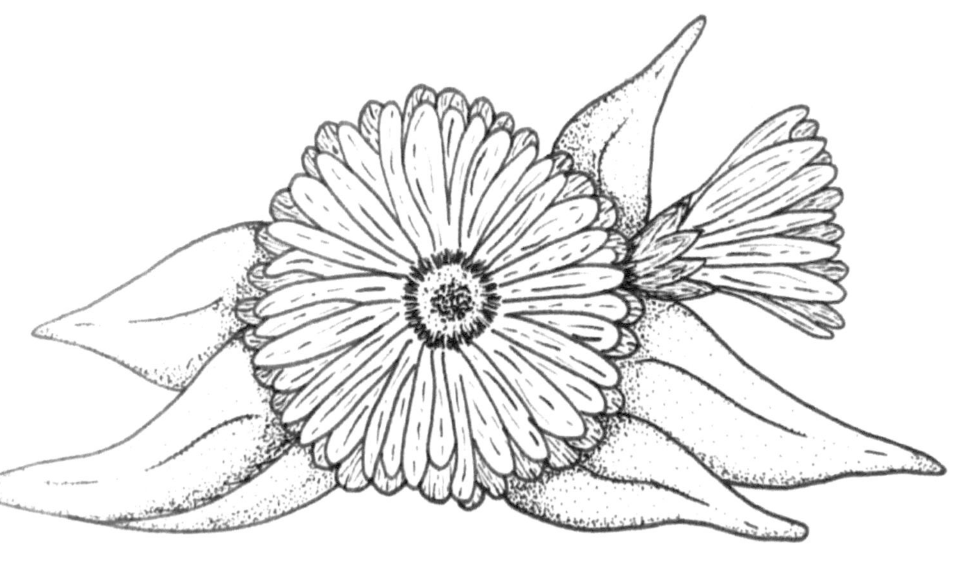

Family: Asteraceae
Genus: Calendula
Species: C. officinalis

My gentleness is healing.

Show me how to reclaim
The energy within.
Teach me how to flourish.
Shine on me and
Warm my bones,
So I may move
These dams built by fear.
Instill in me the ease
Of living and prosperity.
Give me opportunity, health, and
Wealth. I am listening.
I see you in your strength.
I see you growing in
Your fire. I am
Growing in mine too.

# California Poppy

Family: Papaveraceae
Genus: Eschscholzia
Species: E. californica

Rest is essential to dream.

Dance with moon
Sing me into oblivion
Lay me down for my
Eternal sleep

# Chamomile

Family: Asteraceae
Genus: Matricaria
Species: M. chamomilla

I deserve peace.

To the racing and fearful heart,
Chamomile smiles
And whispers
Sweet songs of understanding.

# Chickweed

Family: Caryophyllaceae
Genus: Stellaria
Species: S. media

I grow in supportive environments.

All I see is white
And bleak.
My feet are cold from sinking.
Desolation
Hangs stale in the air,
But I sense you underfoot.
I will dig, bare-handed and frozen,
Hopeful,
Until the stars come home
In spring.

Family: Asteraceae
Genus: Taraxacum
Species: T. officinale

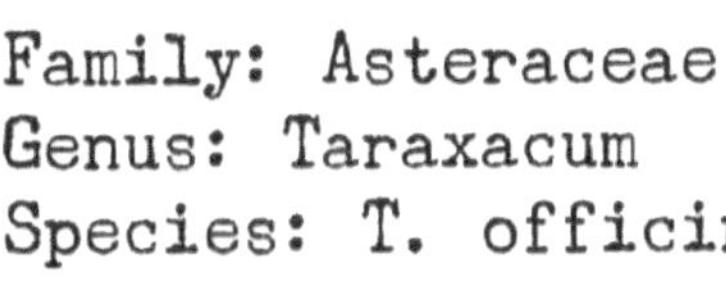

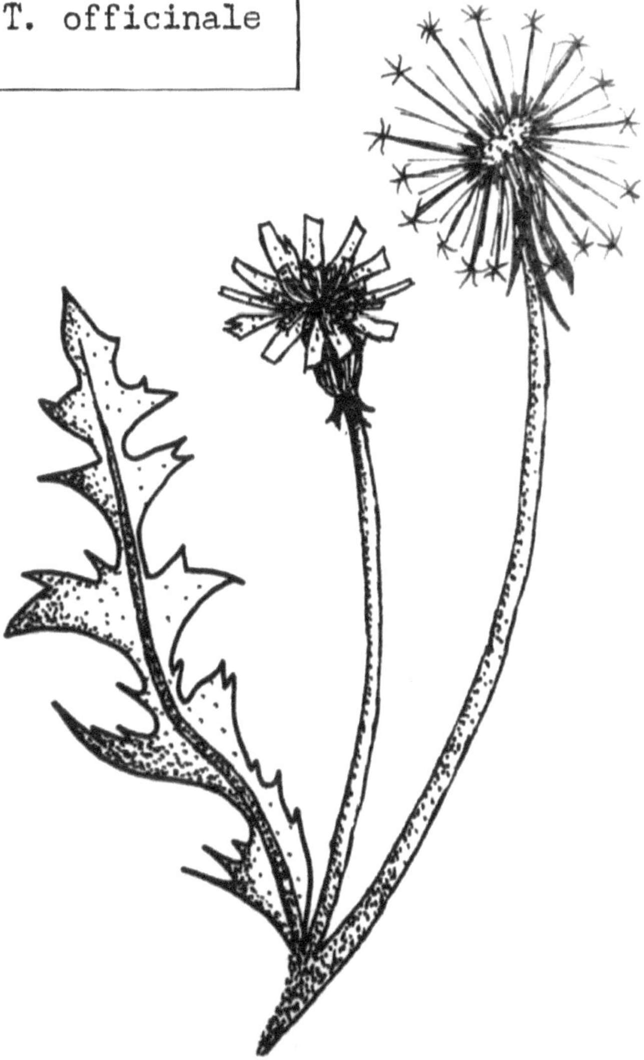

# *Dandelion*

I know my worth, and I am invaluable.

In a world where poison is prized,

Taken to endure the day,

You extend your hand

To those to numb to feel you reaching.

You yell your worth

To those learned deaf to your language.

You are everywhere,

Yet nowhere at all.

You must be furious,

But you persist,

So, in the end,

You must be love.

# Datura

Family: Solanaceae
Genus: Datura
Species: D. stramonium

My experiences provide opportunity
for liberation.

Darkness and desolation
Pave the road to enlightenment.
Escape is the ultimate release;
Forgetting to unfeel.
Once I take you in,
Skin soaked, toxic,
I won't stop until I
Reach the light.
I won't stop until I
Become everything
I should have been all along.
Let me go.

# Dead Nettle

Family: Lamiaceae
Genus: Lamium
Species: L. purpureum

I choose to show up, grow, and
create beauty in the most barren soils,
even after the darkest winters.

In disturbed soils between the grasses,
Where no one else dare go,
You nestle in the first of spring
And smile with your bloom.
Soft purple hued patches
Welcome bare feet,
And hands, and knees, and wake
The sleeping bees.
Tenacity and hope
Bring beauty and life
To what once was, to our simple eyes,
Dull and lifeless dead dirt.

Elder

I am powerful because of both my strength and my softness.

Sweet elder,
Deep magick,
Transform my searching soul,
Guide and heal
As I fall through the threshold and
Stumble upon fate.
Mother goddess,
Advise and draw me into the way.
Take my hand,
Pull me astray,
Forgive my mistakes
And my past.
Reflect to me my
Life of wrongs and rights;
Hold the mirror to my nose.
I accept your invitation.
I accept my path from here.
I see your wisdom
Of beginning with the end.
I see you
Reaching out to lead me.
I see you
Walking me home.

# Foxglove

Family: Plantaginaceae
Genus: Digitalis
Species: D. purpurea

*I improve the lives of those around me.*

$T$ake her gently,

She dreams in black.

With gifts of whispers and

Sincere wishes, she wraps around the heart.

She offers a taste of strength;

Reviving hearts barely beating.

But careful of her

Bitter tongue. She bites

The life that grabs.

So quick to breathe in the dark

When love is blinded

By carelessness and greed,

She licks her lips and lavishly dines

On last exhale.

# Hawthorn

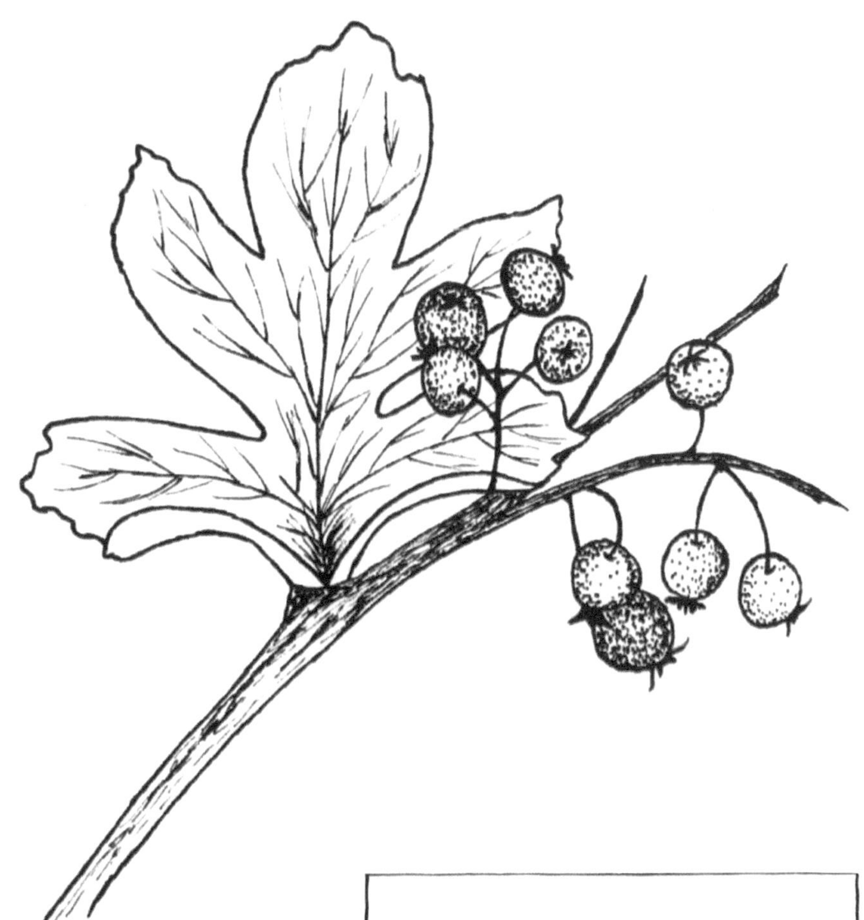

Family: Rosaceae
Genus: Crataegus
Species: C. monogyna

Like cooling waters,
I will keep flowing.

I have cried out
From the depths of heartaches
That never subside.
I have felt the weight
Of emptiness residing
In the places meant
To keep love's secrets.
I have tripped and fallen
And stumbled onto your thorn
Only to be embraced.
I have inhaled your sweetness
When all I had to drink
Was bitter poison.
I have tasted your fruits;
Your rhythm beats within me.
I may be broken,
But I am not without hope.

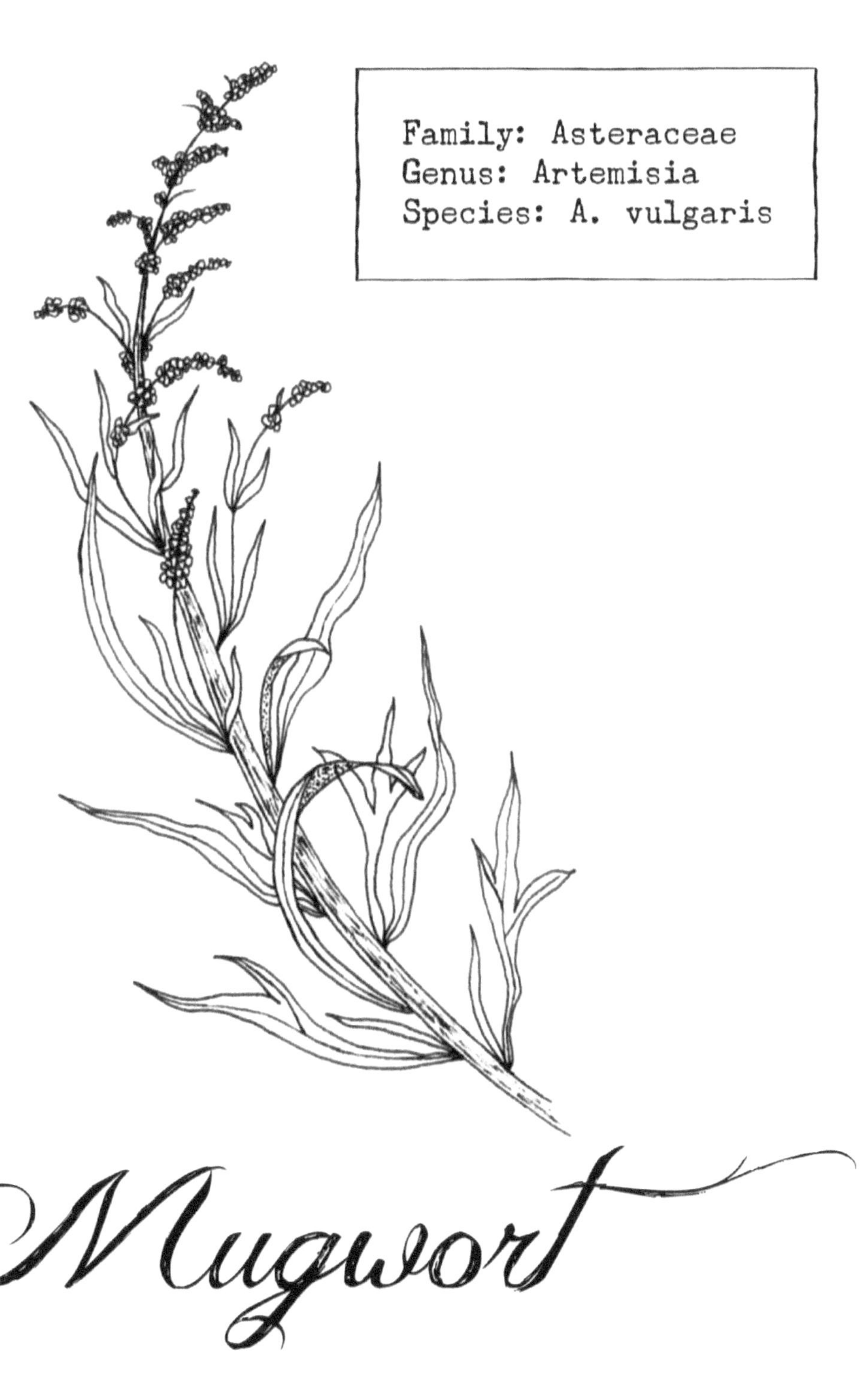

Family: Asteraceae
Genus: Artemisia
Species: A. vulgaris
Mugwort

I am open to and trust my intuition.

I followed you here
To follow my dreams,
But you had other plans.
I woke drunk with your promise
After I laid in your bed,
Unaware of you watching me sleep.
I gave you my word,
A piece of my heart;
I placed it at your feet.
I took you in gently
And wrapped you in braids;
You filled my mind with smoke.
I left you for love,
But love never came,
And now I'm left lonely and crying for you.

# Mullein

Family: Scrophularieae
Genus: Verbascum
Species: V. thapsus

I illuminate my path with every breath I take.

Cover me in hot wax,
And light me on fire;
I won't feel a thing.
With this flame as my guide,
I take to the night
In search of my only desire.
I've loved you since the moment
I saw you; I can't help
But cry out your name.
There is nothing that can hurt me,
Not sickness, not death,
No, not even this flame.
Your absence is my only pain.

# Queen Anne's Lace

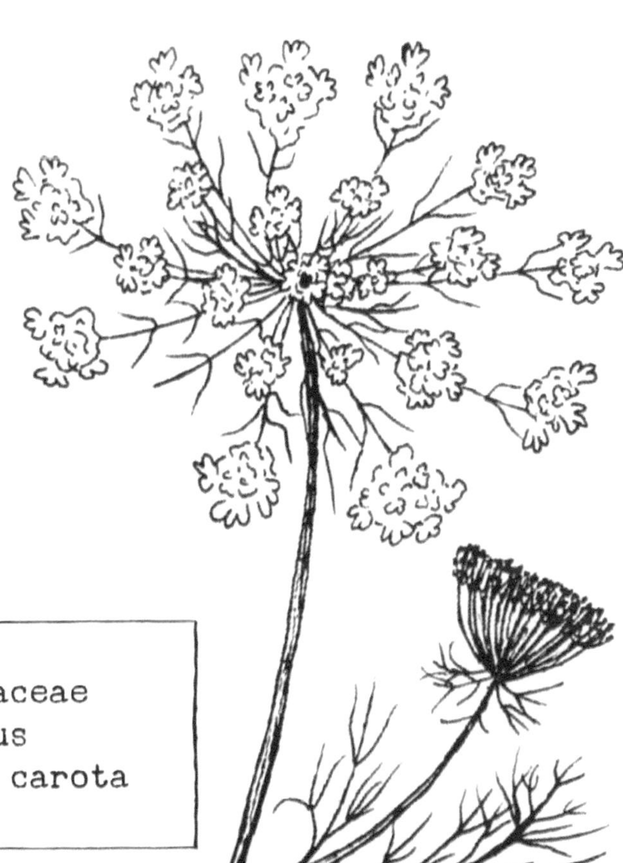

Family: Apiaceae
Genus: Daucus
Species: D. carota

I take refuge in my wildness.

To be a queen among,
To take rightfully
That which is fundamental to your being,
Soul essence.
Survival.
To stand out proud;
Reclamation with grandeur.
Inherit the dirt, and sweat, and toil.
Be one with the whole,
Fulfill and follow your purpose.
The greater good, a common goal.
To be wild and free.

St. John's Wort

I am healing my wounds,
inside and out.

I am not afraid
Of the evil in the world.
I am not afraid
Of the snake's venom.
I am not afraid
Of the demons that occupy my mind,
Or the spirits that stir my soul.
I reach tall, as you do,
To harness the sun's bounty.
I paint my face red
With the blood of your bud.
I am not afraid
Of the war.
I am ready
For the exorcism of my thoughts.
Shine your light in me.

# Wild Rose

Family: Rosaceae
Genus: Rosa
Species: R. multiflora

My love is worth the fight.

I'm growing thorns around my heart
To hide the darkness left in ash.
I'm growing thorns around my heart
To protect the fragile soil.
I'm growing thorns around my heart
To shelter from the storms.
I'm growing thorns around my heart
To keep my wolves and seedlings warm.
I'm growing thorns around my heart
To caution and take care.
I'm growing thorns around my heart,
But I'm growing love and wild roses too.

# Willow

Family: Salicaceae
Genus: Salix
Species: S. nigra

I remain rooted and stable, through floods and toxicity.

Be like the willow,
I heard the wind whisper.
Be soft and gentle,
And move with grace.
Allow yourself to bend;
Be flexible and give.
Set root in murky waters,
And grow with every rain.
Be like the willow,
For she is hard to break.

Wormwood

I am beautifully misunderstood.

Dance naked
With me in the moonlight,
Silvery and scant.
I am intoxicated by you.
Your scent
Hovers like a thick fog,
Enveloping and eerie.
I drink you in.
Tell me all
The fiery secrets that you keep
Heavy and hidden.
I am yours, but only for the night.

# Yarrow

Family: Asteraceae
Genus: Achillea
Species: A. millefolium

I have endured that which would
leave many weary and withered, but
here I am, blooming.

Slow down.
Deep wounds
Deserve careful intention.
Their gaping darkness
Gushes and exposes
Our most vulnerable pieces.
Slow down.
Healing,
Protected and lasting, is
Created with the energy
Drawn and stored within
For the bleakness of our deserts.
Slow down.
Pick me.
Place me on your pain.
My intention is love, and I am here
To stop a bleeding heart,
And to mend a broken soul.